Mr. Mistoffelees

with

Mungojerrie and Rumpelteazer

Mr. Mistoffelees

with

Mungojerrie and Rumpelteazer

BY T. S. Eliot

WITH PICTURES BY Errol Le Cain

Harcourt Brace Jovanovich, Publishers/Farrar Straus & Giroux, Inc.

Mr. Mistoffelees

You ought to know Mr. Mistoffelees!
The Original Conjuring Cat —
(There can be no doubt about that).
Please listen to me and don't scoff. All his
Inventions are off his own bat.

There's no such Cat in the metropolis;
He holds all the patent monopolies
For performing surprising illusions
And creating eccentric confusions.
   At prestidigitation
      And at legerdemain
   He'll defy examination
      And deceive you again.

The greatest magicians have something to learn
From Mr. Mistoffelees' Conjuring Turn.
Presto!
     Away we go!
          And we all say: OH!
               Well I never!
               Was there ever
               A Cat so clever
                    As Magical Mr. Mistoffelees!

He is quiet and small, he is black
From his ears to the tip of his tail;
He can creep through the tiniest crack
He can walk on the narrowest rail.
He can pick any card from a pack,
He is equally cunning with dice;
He is always deceiving you into believing
That he's only hunting for mice.

He can play any trick with a cork
    Or a spoon and a bit of fish-paste;
If you look for a knife or a fork
    And you think it is merely misplaced—
You have seen it one moment, and then it is *gawn*!
But you'll find it next week lying out on the lawn.
    And we all say: OH!
        Well I never!
        Was there ever
        A Cat so clever
            As Magical Mr. Mistoffelees!

His manner is vague and aloof,
You would think there was nobody shyer —
But his voice has been heard on the roof
When he was curled up by the fire.
And he's sometimes been heard by the fire
When he was about on the roof —
(At least we all *heard* somebody who purred)

Which is incontestable proof
   Of his singular magical powers:
      And I have known the family to call
   Him in from the garden for hours,
      While he was asleep in the hall.
And not long ago this phenomenal Cat
Produced *seven kittens* right out of a hat!

And we all said: OH!
Well I never!
Did you ever
Know a Cat so clever
As Magical Mr. Mistoffelees!

Mungojerrie and Rumpelteazer

Mungojerrie and Rumpelteazer were a very notorious couple of cats.
As knockabout clowns, quick-change comedians, tight-rope walkers and
  acrobats
They had an extensive reputation. They made their home in Victoria Grove —
That was merely their centre of operation, for they were incurably given to
  rove.
They were very well known in Cornwall Gardens, in Launceston Place and in
  Kensington Square —
They had really a little more reputation than a couple of cats can very well
  bear.

If the area window was found ajar
And the basement looked like a field of war,
If a tile or two came loose on the roof,
Which presently ceased to be waterproof,
If the drawers were pulled out from the bedroom chests,
And you couldn't find one of your winter vests,
Or after supper one of the girls
Suddenly missed her Woolworth pearls:
Then the family would say: "It's that horrible cat!
It was Mungojerrie — or Rumpelteazer!" — And most of the time they left it at
　　that.

Mungojerrie and Rumpelteazer had a very unusual gift of the gab.

They were highly efficient cat-burglars as well, and remarkably smart at a
    smash-and-grab.

They made their home in Victoria Grove. They had no regular occupation.

They were plausible fellows, and liked to engage a friendly policeman in
    conversation.

    When the family assembled for Sunday dinner,

    With their minds made up that they wouldn't get thinner

    On Argentine joint, potatoes and greens,

    And the cook would appear from behind the scenes

    And say in a voice that was broken with sorrow:

    "I'm afraid you must wait and have dinner *tomorrow*!

    For the joint has gone from the oven — like that!"

Then the family would say: "It's that horrible cat!

It was Mungojerrie — or Rumpelteazer!" — And most of the time they left it at
    that.

Mungojerrie and Rumpelteazer had a wonderful way of working together.
And some of the time you would say it was luck, and some of the time you
     would say it was weather.
They would go through the house like a hurricane, and no sober person could
     take his oath.
Was it Mungojerrie — or Rumpelteazer? or could you have sworn that it
     mightn't be both?

     And when you heard a dining-room smash
     Or up from the pantry there came a loud crash
     Or down from the library came a loud *ping*
     From a vase which was commonly said to be Ming —
Then the family would say: "Now which was which cat?
It was Mungojerrie! AND Rumpelteazer!" — And there's nothing at all to be
     done about that!

First published in 1990 by Faber and Faber Limited, London

Library of Congress Cataloging-in-Publication Data
Eliot, T. S. (Thomas Stearns), 1888–1965.
Mr. Mistoffelees, with Mungojerrie and Rumpelteazer/by T. S. Eliot;
with pictures by Errol Le Cain.
p.   cm.
Two poems from his Old Possum's book of practical cats.
ISBN 0-15-256230-3
1. Cats — Poetry. I. Le Cain, Errol. II. Eliot, T. S. (Thomas Stearns), 1888–1965.
Old Possum's book of practical cats. III. Title. IV. Title: Mister Mistoffelees,
with Mungojerrie and Rumpelteazer.
PS3509.L43A6   1991
821′.912 — dc20   90-39856
Printed in Great Britain
First U.S. edition 1991
A B C D E